D1049984

scary clowns

Andrews McMeel
Publishing

Kansas City

INTRODUCTION

The clown is an ancient character of entertainment, universally recognized and easily understood since his whole act consists of slapstick. A clown doesn't tell jokes; he is one. A clown is silent, yet his physical appearance and actions scream with exaggeration and threat. Clowns of every nationality, from American and European to African, Russian, and Chinese, fall over, throw things at each other, play with knives, walk high wires, tumble, gurn (make grotesque faces), and collapse. A clown can "die" several times in an act only to rise again, a silent smile across his painted face. Only the great Wile E. Coyote can match a clown's persistence and resistance to death.

The tradition and art of clowning found its way around the world via circuses, in traveling troupes of players or in solo performance, with each culture adding to and subtracting from the clown's classic repertoire of tricks, pratfalls, and moves. From sinister beginnings in medieval plays, the clown developed into a benign character, and for centuries they were considered good, clean fun, suitable for all ages, from toddler to retiree.

Clowns helped establish the Hollywood film-making tradition. Charlie Chaplin, Max Sennett, Harold Lloyd, Laurel and Hardy, Harry Langdon, and the Keystone Kops were all great physical, slapstick comedians—clowns made stars by the silent screen. Clowns continued to tour throughout the first half of the twentieth century, with circuses and on vaudeville stages. With the advent of television, some even made it onto the small screen well into the 1950s. Smokey Robinson made a soul icon out of clowns (*Tears of a Clown*); in the mid-1960s the infamous San Francisco Mime Troupe made clowning a political statement, and in 1964 the largest fast-food franchise in the world adopted a clown as their mascot. Ronald McDonald became the symbol of wholesome family fun.

And then, something happened. People became scared of clowns.

The term *coulrophobia*—fear of clowns—has come into common usage only in the past two decades. Now there are numerous support groups and hundreds of Web sites dedicated to the fear. "I Hate Clowns" sites encourage people to share their fear and hatred online. There is a Web site dedicated to real anti-clown news, which is full of stories concerning clowns who have abused children, stolen things, killed, robbed banks, or defrauded normal, God-fearing people. You can buy anti-clown T-shirts, pins, cards, and hats. There are coulrophobic blogs and therapy courses. And they don't all originate in America. There are British, German, Scandinavian, and Eastern European anti-clown Web sites.

Part of the rise of coulrophobia can be blamed on the increasing use of clowns in slasher horror films. Since the early 1980s, a string of movies has been made in which the central, murderous character is a clown. These include *Killjoy* and *Killjoy 2*; *The Clowns*; *S.I.C.K.*; *The Clown at Midnight*; *The Funhouse*; *Clownhouse*; Stephen King's *It*; *Killer Klowns from Outer Space*; *Shakes the Clown* (about an alcoholic clown); and *A Clown in Babylon*. Not that the idea was new. In 1924, the classic horror movie actor Lon Chaney played a clown in *He Who Gets Slapped*. Four years later he reprised the role in *Laugh, Clown, Laugh*.

Perhaps the 1980s wave of killer clown movies was "inspired" by the acts of one of America's most notorious serial killers, John Wayne Gacy. Between 1972 and 1979, Gacy raped, tortured, and murdered thirty-three young men, many of whom he buried under his house in Chicago. When news of Gacy's crimes hit the news, they were often illustrated using a black and white photograph of the killer dressed in full clown garb and makeup. He had volunteered several times to act as a children's entertainer for a charity he worked for during the period that he was committing his horrendous crimes. Between his conviction in 1982 and his death by lethal injection in 1994, Gacy slipped several of his own drawings and paintings out of prison. Most featured a clown somewhere in them.

For many people who suffer from coulrophobia, though, it seems that their fear began as children when confronted by a grotesquely made-up man wearing over-large trousers, shoes, and red nose in the semidarkness of a circus tent. For others there seems to be no rational reason for what is an uncommonly irrational fear. Perhaps it's simply that for most eager conformists, the idea of a man (although there are female clowns, of course) willingly turning himself into an ugly, different, figure of ridicule is too scary to contemplate.

There is undoubtedly an element of irony apparent on many

anti-clown Web sites. The idea of turning a childish, simple figure of fun into a demonic, murdering, scary monster reveals a familiar pubescent tendency to see the world as a frightening place. This can help explain the existence of the El Salvadorian street gangs who rob, murder, and maim each other while dressed as clowns, and David LaChapelle's movie *Rize*. In it Tommy the Clown, a Compton homeboy who dresses like a clown and invents a dance craze called Krumping, shows off a new way to keep kids out of gangs. He and his crew have also starred in various hip-hop videos, projecting the image of clowns as mean muthas.

There is no doubt that hundreds of thousands of people suffer from a genuine fear of clowns. This book does not attempt to analyze coulrophobia. In fact, it makes no comment about scary clowns at all. It is simply a catalog of some of the scariest clown images that exist. The images are from different times and countries. They are of performers, actors, and professional and amateur clowns. To many viewers some of the images may not seem scary at all. But for too many people these images are more than scary— they are horrific. This book is for them.

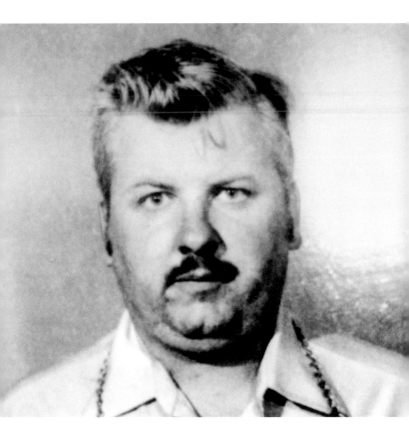

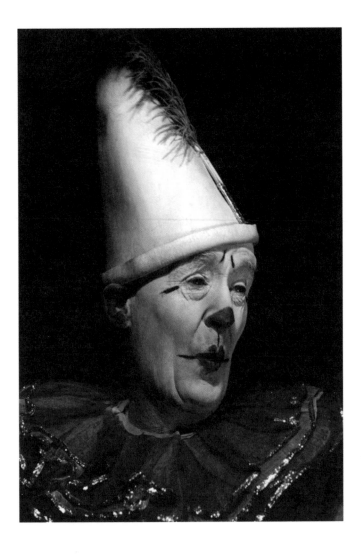

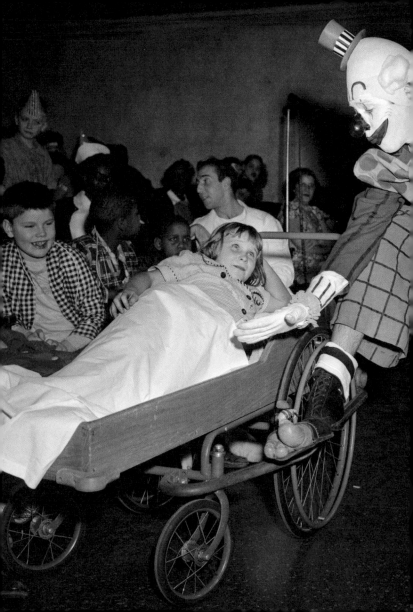

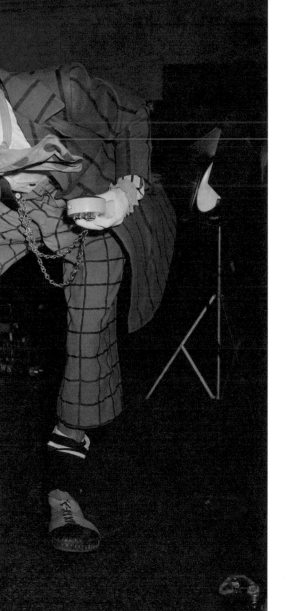

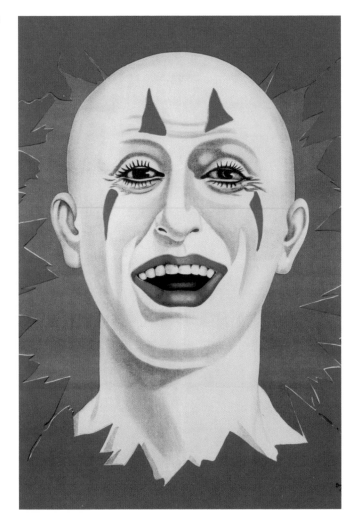

54

60

1844-28 AD

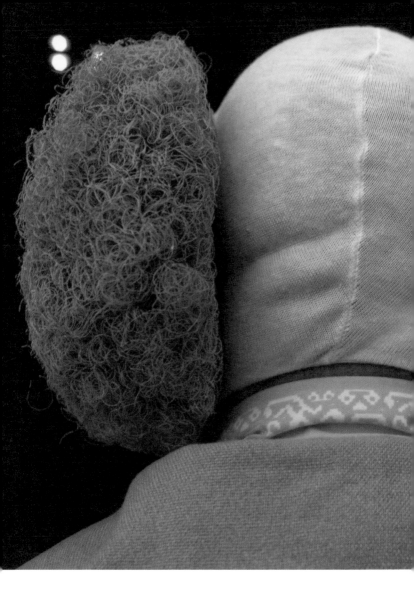

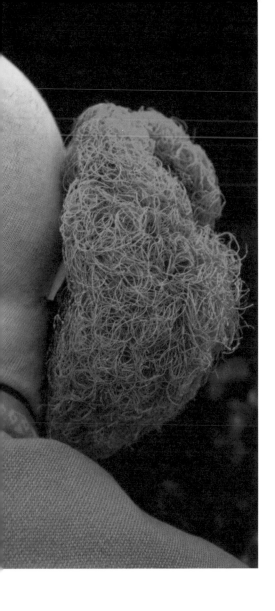

PICTURE CAPTIONS and CREDITS

Cover 1930s clown poster.
Swim Ink 2, LLC/Corbis

Pages 10–11 Italian clowns, father
and son Luigi and Auguste Falco,
in Venice, Italy, 1994.
Arne Hodalic/Corbis

Page 12 Lon Chaney as "He" in
the 1924 MGM silent movie *He
Who Gets Slapped*.
Bettmann/Corbis

Page 13 A police photo of serial
killer John Wayne Gacy taken when
he was in custody for questioning
in connection with the discovery of
five decomposed bodies found in
the crawl space of a house he
owned. On weekends Gacy would
often dress as a clown and
entertain local children. While on
death row awaiting execution Gacy
created several paintings of
clowns. Chicago, Illinois, 1978.
Bettmann/Corbis

Page 14 Actor Brian Dennehy in
clown makeup as John Wayne
Gacy in a TV movie of the serial
killer's life, Los Angeles, 1992.
Corbis Sygma

Page 15 Lou Jacobs and
Knucklehead the Chihuahua, New
York, New York, 1979.
Bettmann/Corbis

Pages 16–17 Tinkertoys and
Clown, by Charles Bell, 1982.
Louis K. Meisel Gallery, Inc./Corbis

Pages 18–19 A child wearing a
clown mask at a clown festival in
Basel, Switzerland, 2001.
Lindsay Hebberd/Corbis

Page 20 A clown in traditional
Comedia Del Arte-style hat and
makeup. The ruff and makeup bear
strong resemblances to those
adopted by mime artists in the
20th century. Undated.
Hulton-Deutsch Collection/Corbis

Page 21 The great French pantomimist Pilar Morin, photographed by the almost equally famous B. J. Falk. Probably in New York, ca. 1907.
Corbis

Page 22 Smoky the Clown shows a group of children how he applies his makeup. Smoky usually shows children how to be clowns.
Photograph by Frank Pocklington, Ramsgate, Kent, England, 1956.
Hulton-Deutsch Collection/Corbis,

Page 23 Emmett Kelly as Weary Willie, the sad hobo clown, 1940s.
Underwood & Underwood/Corbis

Pages 24–25 Clowns are role models for members of the Mara Salvatrucha in El Salvador, because they represent, "the man who cries and laughs." Gang members often have clowns tattooed on their bodies. Photograph taken at Quezaltepeque Penitentiary, El Salvador, 2004.
Christian Poveda/Corbis

Pages 26–27 Three Mexican clowns on December 10, the Mexican Day of the Clowns. Mexico City, 1999.
Reuters/Corbis

Page 28 Petey the Clown has been a performer in the outdoor amusement business all of his life. He began in the 1940s with the Ringling Bros. and Barnum & Bailey Circus, Logan, Pennsylvania, 1995.
Brenda Ann Kenneally/Corbis

Page 29 Koke helps to make up Harti, dressed as a mother, before a circus show in London, 1951.
Hulton-Deutsch Collection/Corbis

Pages 30–31 The clown room at the Circus World Museum, in Baraboo, Wisconsin, 1996.
Layne Kennedy/Corbis

Page 32 Henry Fonda (left) and Emmett Kelly pose together to publicize the General Electric Theater presentation on CBS television of Kelly's autobiography. New York, New York, 1955.
Bettmann/Corbis

Page 33 A clown with the Lias Clown Troupe, photographed by the renowned Edwardian society photographer E. O. Hoppe in Australia. Probably 1930s.
E. O. Hoppe/Corbis

Page 34 Soviet clown Yuri Kuklachev, founder and patron of the world's only Cat Theater, Moscow, Russia, 1996.
Eric Roberts/Corbis Sygma

Page 35 A clown at the famous Ringling Bros. and Barnum & Bailey Circus, 1981.
Bob Krist/Corbis

Pages 36–37 A patient of the psychiatric hospital of Havana, Cuba, dressed as a clown. Hospital staff and volunteers organized a carnival for their approximately 3,000 live-in and outpatients to mark the end of Carnival. Havana, Cuba, 2003.
Claudia Daut/Corbis

Pages 38–39 A clown with a mad grin drags a child between parked cars, 1959.
Jack Moebes/Corbis

Page 40 A clown ball toss game. The object is to get a ball into the clown's mouth, for which you win a prize, 2001.
George B. Diebold/Corbis

Page 41 Clarabell, star of the beloved 1950s television series *Howdy Doody Show*, carrying a sign bearing his name.
Bettmann/Corbis

Page 42 Little Pipo II, 5 ½-year-old son of famed French clown Pipo, applies makeup before taking to the sawdust at the Medrano Circus with his father. Paris, France, 1954.
Bettmann/Corbis

Page 43 Cigar Store Harlequin. Manhattan, New York, ca. 1910. Photo Collection Alexander Alland, Sr./Corbis

Page 44–45 Actor Jimmy Stewart garbed in the role of "Buttons" the clown from the movie *The Greatest Show on Earth* entertains some Bellevue patients. New York, New York, 1952. Bettmann/Corbis

Page 46–47 A group of clowns. Bognor Regis, England, ca. 1989. Cordaiy Photo Library Ltd./Corbis

Page 48 "America's Best Known Clown," Emmett Kelly, 1947. Bettmann/Corbis

Page 49 Rock performer Alice Cooper performing in macabre clown eye makeup, 1985. Neal Preston/Corbis

Pages 50–51 Over 2,400 clowns marched in the Sesimbra (Portugal) Carnival to set a world record for clown parades, 2003. Reuters/Corbis

Page 52 Blinko (left) and Frankie Saluto plant flowers in the Channel Garden at the Rockefeller Center, New York, New York, 1960. Bettmann/Corbis

Page 53 A movie clown of the 1950s. Sunset Boulevard/Corbis

Page 54 A stock clown head poster design, 1930s. Swim Ink 2, LLC/Corbis

Page 55 American clown and writer Howard Butten, aka Buffo, plays his miniature violin. Paris, France, 1999. Eric Robert/Corbis

Pages 56–57 Clowns Billy Denaro and E. Guillanme Polidor (kneeling) "entertain" kids of the Home for Destitute Crippled Children of Chicago, Illinois, ca. 1910. Underwood & Underwood/Corbis

Pages 58–59 Female clowns celebrate Welberfastnacht, the day of the Cologne Festival when women take control, 2001. Reuters/Corbis

Page 60 (left to right) Willie Youmans, Frank Theriauh, and Andrew J. Rose publicize the changing of the season and setting of standard time in Chicago, Illinois, 1985.
Bettmann/Corbis

Page 61 Clown Hall of Fame member Paul Jerome in costume, during the 1960s.
Bettmann/Corbis

Pages 62–63 Russian clown Slava Poulin (left) and a troupe member rehearse before *Snowstorm* at the Hackney Theater, London, 1996.
Gideon Mendel/Corbis

Pages 64–65 1930s clown poster.
Swim Ink 2, LLC/Corbis

Page 66 A "children's" night light, 2001.
FK Photo/Corbis

Page 67 Cartoonist Mark Christiansen auditioning for the role of Bozo the Clown, 1993.
Steve Starr/Corbis

Pages 68–69 Leon McBryde as "Buttons," the Ringling Bros. and Barnum & Bailey circus clown. New York, New York, 1975.
Bettmann/Corbis

Pages 70–71 Antiguan clowns, probably 1950s, photographed by American news photographer Bradley Smith (1910–1997).
Bradley Smith/Corbis

Page 72 Lon Chaney in makeup for the silent movie *Laugh, Clown, Laugh,* 1928.
Bettmann/Corbis

Page 73 Clowns in full outfit, undated but probably 1940s.
Bettmann/Corbis

Pages 74–75 A bunch of international clowns at the Clown-Around-the-World Festival in Kuala Lumpur, 2004. (Front, left to right) Bruce "Charlie" Johnson of America, Rone and Gigi of Japan. (Back, left to right) Lee Mullally and Richard Snowberg of America and Sam Tee of Malaysia.
Zainal Abd Halim/Corbis

Page 76 A smiling clown outside the tents of Circus Vargas, Los Angeles, California, 1976.
Henry Dilitz/Corbis

Page 77 A clown of the Bertram Mills Circus, England, 1950s.
Hulton-Deutsch Collection/Corbis

Page 78 Peanuts the clown and fellow performer relax before a show, 1972.
Jonathan Blair/Corbis

Page 79 A small circus on the outskirts of Paris, France, 1999.
Peter Turnley/Corbis

Pages 80–81 A clown with a pig "entertains" children, 1961.
Jack Moebes/Corbis

Pages 82–83 A biker clown rides through the 31st Annual Halloween Parade in New York, New York, 2004.
Ramin Talaie/Corbis

Page 84 Clowns at the Hoxie Brothers Circus in Millen, Georgia, 1971.
Jonathan Blair/Corbis

Page 85 A child sits with a Ronald McDonald statue outside a Beijing McDonald's, China, 1990.
Joseph Sohm; ChromoSohm Inc./Corbis

Page 86 An early protrait of a clown, ca. 1910.
Bettmann/Corbis

Page 87 Clowns of the German International Circus in Rome, Italy, 1961.
Bettmann/Corbis

Pages 88–89 Tin toy versions of Emmett Kelly as Weary Willie and friends, by Charles Bell, 1950s.
Louis K. Meisel Gallery, Inc./Corbis

Pages 90–91 Stebbo, Stirling, and Bannock of the Yankee Doodle Circus, performing in the UK for Salute the Soldier Week, Windsor, Berkshire, 1944.
Hulton-Deutsch Collection/Corbis

Page 92 "Mr. Jellybeans" Paul
Locley outside a circus tent in
Minchinburg, Australia, 1995.
Paul A. Souders/Corbis

Page 93 Corporate clown, 2000.
Jose Luis Pelaez, Inc./Corbis

Pages 94–95 German clown
Bernhard Paul as a king,
Dusseldorf, Germany, 1994.
Arne Hodalic/Corbis

Page 96 Beckett plays Cheerful
Charlie at the Olympia Circus,
London, England, 1930s.
Hulton-Deutsche Collection/Corbis

Page 97 Clowns resting after a
Christmas show at Crystal Palace,
London, England, 1921.
Hulton-Deutsche Collection/Corbis

Pages 98–99 Characters from the
movie *Man of a Thousand Faces*,
in which James Cagney played Lon
Chaney, whose life was the subject
of the film. Los Angeles, California,
1957.
Bettmann/Corbis

Page 100 Actor Jerry Lewis in
clown outfit, Los Angeles,
California, 1954.
Sunset Boulevard/Corbis

Page 101 A street entertainer
blows up a balloon to "entertain"
kids in Vancouver, Canada, 1995.
Gunter Marx Photography/Corbis

Pages 102–103 A clown quietly
smiles as unsuspecting kids gather
around him. Some even sit on his
knee. California, 1950s.
Jack Moebes/Corbis

Page 104 Clowns serve tea at a
party given for children from
Fulham, organized by the local
Bridgeway Club residents'
Association. WWII had only just
ended, there was still rationing in
England, and kids had to put up
with this kind of thing. 1946.
Hulton-Deutsch Collection/Corbis

Page 105 George L. Fox (1825–1877), the greatest clown of the American stage, in his most famous role, Humpty Dumpty, which he performed 1,268 times. Undated photo.
Bettmann/Corbis

Pages 106–107 Proof that the Swiss have a macabre sense of humor. A "clown" at a Shrove Tuesday celebration in Basel, Switzerland, 1990s.
José F. Problette/Corbis

Page 108 A detail showing the head of Punchinello by Bartolomeo Pinelli, 18th century.
Araldo de Luca/Corbis

Page 109 People in clown outfits at the New Orleans Mardi Gras, 1950s.
Bradley Smith/Corbis

Page 110 Peanuts the Clown prepares to perform at the Hoxie Brothers Circus, 1972.
Jonathan Blair/Corbis

Page 111 An annual clown convention in Costa Rica. They gather to analyze new makeup techniques and the clowns' "ethics." San Jose, Costa Rica, 2003.
Reuters/Corbis

Pages 112–113 Alberto Caroli, son of Sandrine Bouglione and Dominico, at Cirque d'Hiver, Paris, France, 2001.
Stephane Cardinale/Corbis

Page 114 A Clown with a rifle. Funny? Maybe in the 1950s.
Bettmann/Corbis

Page 115 Amy Carter, daughter of President Jimmy Carter, accompanies clowns on an egg roll, Washington, D.C., 1977.
Wally McNamee/Corbis

Pages 116–117 Florida, 1973.
Jonathan Blair/Corbis

End papers Clown heads on a rack in the factory, 1950s.
William Gottlieb/Corbis